I
AFFIRM

I
AFFIRM

Monique Payne

ARPress

ARPress
45 Dan Road Suite 5
Canton MA 02021
Hotline: 1(888) 821-0229
Fax: 1(508) 545-7580

Ordering Information:
Quantity sales. Special discounts are available on quantity purchases by corporations, associations, and others. For details, contact the publisher at the address above.

Printed in the United States of America.

ISBN-13:   Softcover   979-8-89356-178-4
                  eBook   979-8-89356-179-1

Library of Congress Control Number: 2024911627

TABLE OF CONTENTS

PREFACE

More than ten years ago I started writing affirmations for my husband's Ministry, Our Fathers Business, a noon day prayer line. I have always believed that the use of affirmations is an effective tool for becoming or having what you desire. However, it wasn't until I base them upon the "Word of God" that I truly experienced their awesome power. I believe that when we speak, and feel with our hearts what we speak, we receive or manifest what we have spoken. Therefore, I suggest you place your name within the affirmations, prayers and scriptures. Replace my shared experiences with your own. Sing and meditate with not only others, but you in mind. I encourage you to make these affirmations and your time with God a truly personal experience. For they will not only enlighten and encourage all believers, they will also inspire, enrich and transform the lives of everyone. Because my background is faith-based, all prayers and testimonies are scriptural.

Furthermore, all presented Biblical writings and footnotes are derived from the Holy Bible, King James Version (KJV). As for the purpose and meaning of my life heretofore and the information presented in this book, I stand firmly upon, "For all the promises of God in him are yes, and in him Amen, unto the glory of God by us," 2 Corinthians 1:20.

I, also, thank the Road Crew, and the late Ruby Hicks who reminded me of my dear mother. Tracy Hill and my daughter Amber Hardin who came along side me and served as editors.

I Make All Things New

God's resurrection power makes all things new every day - *for these 'affirmations' are true and faithful.*

Prayer: Dear Lord,

Help me recall the difference it makes when You are the priority in my morning. Every day awaken me,

Lord, in body and spirit. Increase my desire to meet with You and hear Your words of affirmation,

assurance, and wisdom as they flow into my being. Only then am I prepared to go into my day. Thank

you for your grace and mercy. In Jehovah's name, I pray.

Amen

Affirmation: I was breathing but not alive; My failures, I tried to hide. He called my name, and I ran out of the grave into God's glorious day!

Scripture: "And he that sat upon the throne said, Behold, I make all things new. And he said unto me, Write: for these words are true and faithful."

(Revelation 21:5, KJV)

Motivation

Affirmation: Because I know the truth, I have faith for everything I hope to manifest!

Scripture: *"Now faith is the substance of things hoped for, the evidence of things not seen."*

(Hebrews 11:1, KJV)

Affirmation: I completely understand God's will for me because it is good, pleasing, and perfect!

Scripture: *"And be not conformed to this world: but be ye transformed by the renewing of your mind, that ye may prove what is that good, and acceptable, and perfect, will of God.*

(Romans 12:2, KJV)

Affirmation: I am blessed by God; What a revelation!

Scripture: *"For it is God which worketh in you both to will and to do of his good pleasure."*

(Philippians 2:13, KJV)

Affirmation: Thank you, Lord! I have been made free!

Scripture: *"If the Son therefore shall make you free, ye shall be free indeed."*

(John 8:36, KJV)

Affirmations Inspired by Worship

Affirmation: Father God, help me think, talk, walk, and love like You!

Song: "Walk With You"-Michael Bethany

Affirmation: Lord, give me you! Everything else can wait!

Song: "Give Me You" - Shana Wilson

Affirmation: God, breathe on me again, for in Your presence is where I want to be!

Song: "In Your Presence" - William McDowell - feat. Israel Houghton

Affirmation: Jesus lives so that I can face tomorrow!

Hymn: "Because He Lives" - Bill & Gloria Gaither

Affirmation: When my back is against the wall, Lord, I look to you!

Scripture: *"Put on the whole armor of God, that ye may be able to stand against the wiles of the devil."* (Ephesians 6:12, KJV)

Affirmation: Whatever I need is in the room; God is here!

Scripture: *"And if we know that he hears us, whatsoever we ask, we know that we have the petitions that we desired of him."*

(1 John 5:15, KJV)

Affirmation: Thank you, Lord, for carrying my burdens and covering my shame!

Scripture: *"For my yoke is easy, and my burden is light."*

(Matthew 11:30, KJV)

Affirmation: I am enough!

Scripture: *"See what great love the Father has lavished on us, that we should be called children of God! And that is what we are! The reason the world does not know us is that it did not know him."*

(John 3:1, KJV)

Affirmation: God's power is made perfect in my shortcomings!

Scripture: *"For though I would desire to glory, I shall not be a fool; for I will say the truth: but now I forbear, lest any man should think of me above that which he seeth me to be, or that he heareth of me."*

(2 Corinthians 12:6-7, KJV)

Affirmation: God is about to blow my mind!

Scripture: *"And he said, Abba, Father, all things are possible unto thee; take away this cup from me: nevertheless, not what I will, but what thou wilt."*

 (Mark 14:36, KJV)

Affirmation: I awaken, for God is calling me!

Scripture: *"Wherefore he saith, awake thou that sleepest, and arise from the dead, and Christ shall give thee light."*

(Ephesians 5:14, KJV)

Affirmations and Prayers

Dear Lord,

I will let go of controlling the circumstances of my life and allow you to do your amazing works! You are my strength. No one can do what you do. I will take up my cross daily and follow Christ. I have been standing on your Word for a long time, and I won't give up now. Thank you, Lord! I will get out of my way and follow you.

Amen.

Affirmation: Lord, as I follow you, all things are made new!

Scripture: *"He hath made everything beautiful in his time: also, he hath set the world in their heart so that no man can find out the work that God maketh from the beginning to the end."*

(Ecclesiastes 3:11, KJV)

Affirmation: God's peace gives me an expected end!

Scripture: *"For I know the thoughts that I think toward you, saith the Lord, thoughts of peace, and not of evil, to give you an expected end."*

(Jeremiah 29:11, KJV)

Affirmation: This morning, I align myself with the Holy Spirit, and I began the day with prayer, supplication, and gratitude!

Scripture: *"Be careful for nothing; but in everything by prayer and supplication with thanksgiving let your requests be made known unto God."*

(Philippians 4:6, KJV)

Affirmation: Lord, I thank you for your Spiritual vision, insight, and discernment!

Scripture: *"It is not expedient for me doubtless to glory. I will come to visions and revelations of the Lord."*

(2 Corinthians 12:1, KJV)

Meditate or Sing - I'm Getting Ready

"I'm Getting Ready"

God, You can blow my mind
Hey
'Cause eyes haven't seen
And ears haven't heard
The kind of blessings
The kind of blessings
That's about to follow me
Oh, 'cause victory is here
It kicked defeat out the door
God's doing a new thing, a brand new thing
I'm ready for overflow

God's doing a new thing (yeah)
Get ready for overflow
Yeah, I'm talking to you, I'm talking to you
God's doing a new thing
Get ready for overflow
You been waiting, you been praying, you been pressing, you been fasting
God's doing a new thing
Get ready for overflow
'Cause I'm getting ready to see (yes)
Mm-hmm, something I've never seen
Oh, I'm getting ready to see
Oh-oh
Something I've never seen

Songwriters: Matthew James Redman / Natasha Tameika Cobbs Leonard / Onika Tanya Maraj

Affirmations and Prayers

Dear Lord,

Oh, how I love and trust You for all my needs. You know what is best, and You want to give me everything in accordance with your Word! There is nothing You can't do! With You, all things are possible! I will trust You in every circumstance and with everything that I have. I know that You have put Your Spirit in me for Your glory. As I surrender all, the Holy Spirit empowers me. I am blessed beyond measure with redemption and an inheritance in Christ. Thank you, God!

Amen.

Affirmation: In times like these, I am very sure that my anchor holds!

Scripture: *"Which hope we have as an anchor of the soul, both sure and steadfast, and which entereth into that within the veil."*

(Hebrews 6:19, KJV)

Affirmation: Lord, I am amazed by your wonders! Oh, how you love me!

Scripture: *"And they were all amazed at the mighty power of God. But while they wondered everyone about all the things that Jesus did, he said unto his disciples."*

(Luke 9:43, KJV)

Affirmation: I wait on the Lord and shall continue to wait on him!

Scripture: *"Wait on the Lord: be of good courage, and he shall strengthen thine heart: wait, I say, on the Lord."*

(Psalm 27:14, KJV)

Affirmation: I am kind, Lord; arise in me!

Scripture: *"Arise for our help and redeem us for thy mercies' sake."*

(Psalm 44:26, KJV)

Meditate or Sing - Way Maker

"Way Maker"

Even when I don't see it, You're working

Even when I don't feel it, You're working

My God, You never stop working.

You're the Way maker

My Way maker, Miracle worker, Promise keeper

Light in the darkness, my God

That is who You are.

– Osinachi Kalu Okoro Egbu (Sinach)

Affirmation: I am leaning on God's everlasting arm!

Scripture: "The eternal God is thy refuge, and underneath are the everlasting arms: and he shall thrust out the enemy from before thee; and shall say, Destroy them."

(Deuteronomy 33:27, KJV)

Affirmation: Change me; oh Lord, change me!

Scripture: *"Now unto him that is able to do exceeding abundantly above all that we ask or think, according to the power that worketh in us,"*

(Ephesians 3:20 KJV)

Affirmation: This thorn in my flesh keeps me humble!

Scripture: *"And lest I should be exalted above measure through the abundance of the revelations, there was given to me a thorn in the flesh, the messenger of Satan to buffet me, lest I should be exalted above measure."*

(2 Corinthians 12:7, KJV)

Affirmation: Faithful! Faithful! Faithful is my God!

Scripture: *"If ye abide in me, and my words abide in you, ye shall ask what ye will, and it shall be done unto you."*

(John 15:7 KJV)

Affirmation: I am coming up and on my way to excellence!

Scripture: *"For the good that I would I do not: but the evil which I would not, that I do."*

(Romans 7:19 KJV)

Affirmation: *God loves me and you! Just believe, for we have everlasting life!*

Scripture: *"For God so loved the world, that he gave his only begotten Son, that whosoever believeth in him should not perish, but have everlasting life."*

(John 3:16, KJV)

Reflections

You can write your thoughts here.

_____

_____

_____

_____

_____

_____

_____

_____

_____

_____

_____

_____

_____

_____

_____

_____

_____

_____

_____

_____

_____

Health and Wellness
Quotes

"If you can't fly, then run; if you can't run, then walk; if you can't walk, then crawl, but whatever you do, you have to keep moving forward."

– Dr. Martin Luther King Jr.

"Obstacles don't have to stop you. If you run into a wall, don't turn around and give up. Figure out how to climb it, go through it, or work around it."

-Langston Hughes

"Never be limited by other people's limited imaginations."

—Dr. Mae Jemison, the first African American female astronaut

Affirmations

Affirmation: I live to live and live again!

Scripture: *"But the Comforter, which is the Holy Ghost, whom the Father will send in my name, he shall teach you all things, and bring all things to your remembrance, whatsoever I have said unto you."*

(John 14:26)

Affirmations: God is healing me now!

Scriptures: *"Confess your faults one to another, and pray one for another, that ye may be healed. The effectual fervent prayer of a righteous man availeth much."*

(James 5:16, KJV)

Affirmation: I have the energy and strength to succeed!

Scripture: *"Be of good courage, and he shall strengthen your heart, all ye that hope in the Lord."*

(Psalm 31:24, KJV)

Affirmation: Jehovah Rapha is blessing me now! Yes, now!

Scripture: *"And ye shall serve the Lord your God, and he shall bless thy bread, and thy water, and I will take sickness away from the midst of thee."*

(Exodus 23:25)

Affirmation: I am protected by the Blood of Jesus!

Scripture: *"And, having made peace through the blood of his cross, by him to reconcile all things unto himself; by him, I say, whether they be things in earth or things in heaven."*

(Colossians 1:20, KJV)

Affirmation: Christ knows all of my weaknesses, and I take them to Him in prayer!

Scripture: *"The Spirit of the Lord is upon me, because he hath anointed me to preach the gospel to the poor; he hath sent me to heal the brokenhearted, to preach deliverance to the captives, and recovering of sight to the blind, to set at liberty them that are bruised,"*

(Luke 4:18, KJV)

Testimony - My Life with Multiple Sclerosis

My Life with Multiple Sclerosis

In 2000, I was diagnosed with Multiple Sclerosis (MS). I consider myself fortunate to have had my children before this life-changing disease entered my life. Throughout this book, I will share some of the moments I've experienced, which I call testimonies. My faith and my written affirmations have strengthened me throughout this challenging journey.

For example, during a major flare-up, I spent much of my time confined to bed, unable to do anything. The pain and the physical toll of this disease are beyond words. It also affected my ability to walk; at times, I had to rely on a walker until I regained my mobility. These are just a few ways MS has transformed my daily life.

Even so, I thank God for my strong faith. Even when I couldn't write affirmations or read scripture, His words remained in my heart in one form or another. Life has been challenging, but the enemy never succeeded in keeping me down!

Affirmations and Prayers

Affirmation: I have the victory to live a life of wholeness - Body, Soul, and Spirit!

Scripture: *"I call heaven and earth to record this day against you that I have set before you life and death, blessing and cursing: therefore, choose life, that both thou and thy seed may live:"*

(Deuteronomy 30:19, KJV)

Affirmation: The manifestation of Christ's grace rests upon me!

Scripture: *"And he said unto me, My grace is sufficient for thee: for my strength is made perfect in weakness. Most gladly, therefore, will I rather glory in my infirmities, that the power of Christ may rest upon me."*

(2 Corinthian 12:9, KJV)

Affirmation: By the stripes of Christ, I am made whole!

Scripture: *"Who his own self bare our sins in his own body on the tree, that we, being dead to sins, should live unto righteousness: by whose stripes ye were healed."*

(1 Peter 2:24, KJV)

Affirmation: With wisdom, Jehovah enables me to care for my body!

Scripture: *"Wisdom is the principal thing; therefore get wisdom: and with all thy getting get understanding."*

(Proverbs 4:7, KJV)

Affirmation: Lord, I decree that my healed body be established!

Scripture: *"Thou shalt also decree a thing, and it shall be established unto thee: and the light shall shine upon thy ways."*

(Job 22:28)

Affirmation: I am praising, singing, and still asking, why me, Lord? So much pain, but I have triumphed!

Scripture: *"But the fruit of the Spirit is love, joy, peace, longsuffering, gentleness, goodness, faith, Meekness, temperance: against such there is no law."*

(Galatians 5:22-23, KJV)

Affirmation: The Lord is delivering me, now, from this pain!

Scripture: *"Consider mine affliction, and deliver me Lord!"*

(Psalm 119:153, KJV)

Affirmation: I rebuke lesions, cysts, tumors, kidney failure, high blood pressure, Multiple Sclerosis, Cancer, or any form of sickness in my body!

Scripture: *"But he was wounded for our transgressions, he was bruised for our iniquities: the chastisement of our peace was upon him; and with his stripes we are healed."*

(Isaiah 53:5, KJV)

Affirmation: I am thankful for who I am and whose I am!

Scriptures: *"No weapon that is formed against thee shall prosper; and every tongue that shall rise against thee in judgment thou shalt condemn. This is the heritage of the servants of the Lord, and their righteousness is of me, saith the Lord."*

(Isaiah 54:17, KJV)

Meditate or Sing – No Weapon

"No Weapon"

No Weapon Formed Against Me Shall Prosper

No weapon formed against me shall prosper

It won't work

God will do what he said he would do

He's not a man that he should lie (stand by his word) he will come through

He will stand by his word, he will come through

Oh, I won't be afraid of the arrow by day

From the hand of my enemy

I can stand my ground with the Lord on my side

For the snares they have set will not succeed

No weapon formed against me shall prosper (No way)

It won't work

Don't be afraid of the evils or the snares of my enemies, if you believe it say

There just ain't one (There just ain't one weapon no)

Although they've sent a snare to trap you.

Songwriters: Fred Hammond / Alvin Moor

Affirmations and Prayers

Affirmation: When nothing helped, love lifted me!

Scripture: *"In this was manifested the love of God toward us, because that God sent his only begotten Son into the world, that we might live through"*

(1 John 4:9, KJV)

Affirmation: I am never alone! Christ lives in me!

Scripture: *"A man that hath friends must shew himself friendly: and there is a friend that sticketh closer than a brother."*

(Proverbs 18:24, KJV)

Affirmation: I choose to be positive!

Scriptures: *"Finally, brethren, whatsoever things are true, whatsoever things are honest, whatsoever things are just, whatsoever things are pure, whatsoever things are lovely, whatsoever things are of good report; if there be any virtue, and if there be any praise, think on these things."*

(Philippians 4:8, KJV)

Jehovah Rapha,

I honor You as I rise and declare healing and prosperity. You are my way maker, miracle worker, promise keeper, and the light in the darkness. My God! That is who you are! So, I stand here, in the midst of your miracles and promises, thanking you for making a way for me and allowing the light of health to illuminate me - Body, Soul, and Spirit. And so, it is!

Amen.

Affirmation: I am protected by the Blood of Jesus!

Scripture: *"And, having made peace through the blood of his cross, by him to reconcile all things unto himself; by him, I say, whether they be things in earth, or things in heaven."*

(Colossians 1:20, KJV)

Affirmation: Christ knows all my weaknesses!

Scriptures: *"The Spirit of the Lord is upon me, because he hath anointed me to preach the gospel to the poor; he hath sent me to heal the brokenhearted, to preach deliverance to the captives, and recovering of sight to the blind, to set at liberty them that are bruised."*

(Luke 4:18, KJV)

Affirmation: I have the peace of God!

Scripture: *"Peace I leave with you, my peace I give unto you: not as the world giveth, give I unto you. Let not your heart be troubled, neither let it be afraid."*

(John 14:27, KJV)

Affirmation: The mercy of the Lord is mine forever!

Scripture: *"Thy mercy, O Lord, endureth forever: forsake not the works of thine own hands."*

(Psalm 138:8, KJV)

Testimony – My Hope is in the Lord

My Hope Is in the Lord!

As mentioned before, MS is an extremely painful disease. Sometimes, it takes a while to get back on track. In 2021, during the Christmas holiday season, I became very ill and had to be taken to the hospital. The flare-up was intense. In fact, it was so severe that during my hospitalization, I was given steroid treatment through an IV for three days. Upon release, I began physical therapy because I could no longer move around in the same manner. Now, years later, I am still waiting to be restored entirely. I will wait until my change comes. I will wait on the Lord. I will not give up because it is already done!

My soul, wait thou only upon God.

Affirmations and Prayers

Affirmation: Long life shall be added to me!

Scripture: *"For length of days, and long life, and peace, shall they add to me."*

(Proverbs 3:2, KJV)

Affirmation: Lord, in my hope, suffering ends, and my expectation manifests!

Scripture: *"For surely there is an end, and thine expectation shall not be cut off."*

(Proverbs 23:18, KJV)

Affirmation: I live to declare the works of the Lord!

Scripture: *"I shall not die, but live, and declare the works of the Lord."*

(Psalm 118:17, KJV)

Affirmation: Lord, illuminate my understanding of perfect health!

Scripture: *"The entrance of thy words giveth light; it giveth understanding unto the simple."*

(Psalm 19:130, KJV)

Lord,

You are the light of my life, and you make a way in the darkness. Even when I don't feel well, I am reminded that your grace is sufficient. You are with me always! Every time I call unto you, you answer. Oh, how comforted I am to know that you are here. So, now, Lord, I trust that I am healed. I trust that everything is worked out for my good! I trust that every day, in every way, I am visibly restored to health. In your precious name, I pray and thank you.

Amen.

Affirmation: Lord, help me take one day at a time!

Scripture: *"What? Know ye not that your body is the temple of the Holy Ghost which is in you, which ye have of God, and ye are not your own?" For ye are bought with a price: therefore glorify God in your body, and in your spirit, which are God's."*

(I Corinthians 6:19-20, KJV)

Affirmation: I deserve to live healthily!

Scripture: *"Whether therefore ye eat, or drink, or whatsoever ye do, do all to the glory of God."*

(I Corinthians 10:31, KJV)

Affirmation: I am healthy, happy, and whole!

Scripture: *"It shall be health to thy navel, and marrow to thy bones."*

(Proverbs 3:8, KJV)

Affirmation: I am so grateful that my body is healed!

Scripture: *"A merry heart doeth good like a medicine."*

(Proverbs 17:22, KJV)

Reflections

You can write your thoughts here.

_____

_____

_____

_____

_____

_____

_____

_____

_____

_____

_____

_____

_____

_____

_____

_____

_____

_____

_____

_____

_____

_____

_____

_____

_____

_____

_____

_____

_____

_____

_____

_____

_____

_____

_____

_____

_____

_____

_____

_____

_____

_____

_____

_____

_____
_____
_____
_____
_____
_____
_____
_____
_____
_____
_____
_____
_____
_____
_____
_____
_____
_____
_____
_____
_____
_____
_____
_____

Leadership Testimony

Testimony – Everything Happens for A Reason

Everything Happens for a Reason

At 62, I was fired from my job under false accusations of something I did not do. I felt offended, confused, and deeply embarrassed as if people were laughing at my misfortune. I replayed the situation, trying to make sense of it, but the pieces didn't fit. Friends and colleagues who knew my character offered encouraging words, and while I accepted them with love, my heart remained in turmoil.

I felt utterly lost in what I can only describe as a wilderness experience. Sometimes, it's hard to understand why certain things happen in our lives. I found myself asking, "God, what are You doing?" I longed to be vindicated, but I realized I had to let go before anything else. When I finally surrendered my hurt feelings, the people who had wronged me, and the overwhelming sense of discontent, God stepped in.

I had to come to a place of complete trust, believing wholeheartedly that God was in control. Only then did Jehovah God pour out His favor on me! About five months later, I was rehired, even though I had openly shared that I had been previously fired. A new recruiter contacted me, explaining there was no record of my termination. She even told me that my name had been recommended for rehire. I was in awe—God truly is amazing!

It's easy to get caught up in others' gossip and lies, but when we do, we often view people through the distorted lens of misperception. These voices can drown out God's truth, delaying His healing and answers to our prayers. But when we silence the noise and trust Him fully, we make room for His incredible plans to unfold.

Affirmation and Prayers

Father God ,

Forgive me for entertaining voices you did not send my way. Heal and purify my heart so that I do not hold evil or false perceptions of others. Clarify my vision and open my ears to receive truth and wisdom.

I am breaking down barriers and building bridges through prayer. Yes, God is able to bring me out. I must acknowledge my biases and push past animosities. My heavenly Father help me to show love in all I do and say. Dear Lord I will Recover, Repair, Restore and be Revive. This is my prayer for always.

Amen.

Affirmation: God enables me to think strategically; I am a strategic thinker!

Scripture: *"The thoughts of the diligent tend only to plenteousness; but of everyone that is hasty only to want."*

(Proverbs 21:5, KJV)

Affirmation: My breakthrough has come, and I am rejoicing!

Scripture: *"Then said Jesus to those Jews which believed on him, If ye continue in my word, then are ye my disciples indeed; And ye shall know the truth, and the truth shall make you free."*

(John 8:31-32)

Affirmation: I thank you, God, that all things are working together for my good!

Scripture: *"And we know that all things work together for good to them that love God, to them who are the called according to his purpose."*

(Romans 8:28, KJV)

Affirmation: I am set apart; the Lord hears me when I call!

Scripture: *"But know that the Lord hath set apart him that is godly for himself: the Lord will hear when I call unto him."*

(Psalm 4:3, KJV)

Affirmation: My mind is renewed daily, and I demonstrate the perfect will of God!

Scripture: *"And be not conformed to this world: but be transformed by the renewing of your mind, that ye may prove what is that good, and acceptable, and perfect, will of God."*

(Romans 12:2, KJV)

Affirmation: Today, I receive Godly wisdom and understanding!

Scripture: *"Get wisdom, get understanding: forget it not; neither decline from the words of my mouth."*

(Proverbs 4:5, KJV)

LORD

My steps are ordered in God's / Jesus' name. I move by Divine programming. I meet the right people at the right time, go to the right place at the right time and do the right thing at the right time. I am bold in declaring what I want and I confidently reject what is not Godly. My path is laced with grace as I move from glory to glory. I have unhindered access for whatever resources I need, and it is all in Jesus' name.

Amen

Affirmation: God grants me unhindered access to whatever I need! I align my thoughts and actions with His will!

Scripture: : *"For through him we both have access by one Spirit unto the Father*

(Ephesians 2:18)

Affirmation: I am a leader with the confidence to stand alone!

Scripture: *"And this is the confidence that we have in him, that, if we ask anything according to his will,*

he heareth us."

(1 John 5:14, KJV)

Affirmation: I confess It! I believe it! I see it! I live it!

Scripture: *"And be not conformed to this world: but be transformed by the renewing of your mind, that ye may prove what is that good, and acceptable, and perfect, will of God."*

(Romans 12:2, KJV)

Affirmation: My faith removes mountains!

Scripture: *"And Jesus said unto them, Because of your unbelief: for verily I say unto you, If ye have faith as a grain of mustard seed, ye shall say unto this mountain, Remove hence to yonder place; and it shall remove; and nothing shall be impossible unto you."*

(Matthew 17:20, KJV)

Affirmation: I Command My Day!

WELCOME every morning with a smile. LOOK on the new day as another special gift from your GOD, another golden OPPORTUNITY to complete what you were unable to finish yesterday. Be a self-starter.

LET your first hour set the theme of SUCCESS and POSITIVE action that is certain to echo through your entire day. TODAY will never happen again. DO NOT WASTE it with a false start or no start at all. YOU WERE BORN NOT TO FAIL!"

-Og Mandino

Affirmation: Lord, use me as a vessel of grace!

Scripture: *"The Lord is my strength and my shield; my heart trusted in him, and I am helped: therefore my heart greatly rejoiceth; and with my song will I praise him."*

(Psalm 28:7, KJV)

Affirmation: I live outside of disappointment and discouragement!

Scripture: *"How God anointed Jesus of Nazareth with the Holy Ghost and with power: who went about doing good, and healing all that were oppressed of the devil; for God was with him."*

(Acts 10:38, KJV)

Affirmation: I am humble, so the Lord will hear from heaven and heal my land!

Scripture: *"If my people, which are called by my name, shall humble themselves, and pray, and seek my face, and turn from their wicked ways; then will I hear from heaven, and will forgive their sin, and will heal their land."*

(1 Chronicles 7:14, KJV)

Affirmation: I am creating a legacy that lives forever!

Scripture: *"We will not hide them from their children, shewing to the generation to come the praises of the Lord, and his strength, and his wonderful works that he hath done."*

(Psalm 78:4, KJV)

Meditate or Sing

"Wait on You"

I don't believe in fairytales, I guess I've outgrown them

But that doesn't mean that I don't believe

That there's something bigger than me

'Cause I've seen it in a hospital room

When the doctors said, "Sorry, there's nothing more we can do"

Well, it wasn't through

I've never seen a pot of gold at the end of the rainbow

But I've got a promise I can hold in the middle of the struggle

God, if you said it, You'll perform it

May not be how I want You to

But here's what I'll do

I'm gonna wait on You

I'm gonna wait on You

I've tasted Your goodness

I'll trust in Your promise

I'm gonna wait on You

Yes, I will, yes, I will

Elevation Worship and Maverick City

Affirmations

Affirmation: I watch and pray to avoid entering temptation!

Scripture: *"I Watch and pray, that ye enter not into temptation: the spirit indeed is willing, but the flesh is weak."*

(Matthew 26:41, KJV)

Affirmation: I am swift to hear, slow to speak, and slow to wrath!

Scripture: *"Wherefore, my beloved brethren, let every man be swift to hear, slow to speak, slow to wrath"*

(James 1:19, KJV)

Affirmation: I am God's disciple, bearing good fruit!

Scripture: *"Teach me good judgment and knowledge: for I have believed thy commandments."*

(Psalm 119:66, KJV)

Affirmation: I have victory over the enemy! Man's efforts toward me are pointless!

Scripture: *"In God have I put my trust: I will not be afraid what man can do unto me."*

(Psalm 56:11, KJV)

Affirmation: My Father enlarges my territory!

Scripture: *"And Jabez called on the God of Israel, saying, Oh that thou wouldest bless me indeed, and enlarge my coast, and that thine hand might be with me, and that thou wouldest keep me from evil, that it may not grieve me! And God granted him that which he requested."*

(I Chronicles 4:10, KJV)

Quotes

"If there is no struggle, there is no progress." —Frederick Douglass

"The time is always right to do what is right." —Dr. Martin Luther King, Jr.

"Have a vision. Be demanding." —Colin Powell

Affirmations and Prayers

Lord,

Father, hallowed be your name, your kingdom come. I give you thanks and praise your Holy name.

Look upon me with eyes of mercy. May your hand rest upon me? Allow your life-giving power to flow into every part of my body and into the depths of my soul, repairing, cleansing, and restoring me to wholeness and strength for service in your kingdom.

Amen.

Affirmation: Through Christ Jesus, the peace of God keeps me!

Scripture: *"And the peace of God, which passeth all understanding, shall keep your hearts and minds through Christ Jesus."*

(Philippians 4:7, KJV)

Affirmation: Lord, you are my shield! For your glory my head is lifted!

Scripture: "But *thou, O Lord, art a shield for me; my glory, and the lifter up of mine head."*

(Psalm 3:3, KJV)

Affirmation: I am God's soldier!

Scripture: *"Thou therefore endure hardness, as a good soldier of Jesus Christ."*

(2 Timothy 2:3, KJV)

Affirmation: I rise and make my mark!

Scripture: *"For we are not as many, which corrupt the word of God: but as of sincerity, but as of God, in the sight of God speak we in Christ."*

(2 Corinthians 2:17, KJV)

Affirmation: Lord, as a leader, fill my life so that all they see is You!

Scripture: *"Then spake Jesus again unto them, saying, I am the light of the world: he that followeth me shall not walk in darkness, but shall have the light of life."*

(John 8:12, KJV)

Affirmation: Speak Lord! Speak to me! I hear and follow your voice!

Scripture: *"My sheep hear my voice, and I know them, and they follow me."*

(John 10:27, KJV)

Affirmation: God covers, strengthens, and assists me in all circumstances!

Scripture: *"God is our refuge and strength, a very present help in trouble."*

(Psalm 46:1, KJV)

Affirmation: By faith, I work out my soul's salvation with fear and trembling!

Scripture: *"Wherefore, my beloved, as ye have always obeyed, not as in my presence only, but now much more in my absence, work out your own salvation with fear and trembling."*

(Philippians 2:12, KJV)

Affirmation: I am forgiven and I forgive others!

Scripture: *"And be ye kind one to another, tenderhearted, forgiving one another, even as God for Christ's sake hath forgiven you."*

(Ephesians 4:32, KJV)

Affirmation: Today. I have an opportunity to do good with everyone!

Scripture: *"As we have therefore opportunity, let us do good unto all men, especially unto them who are of the household of faith"*

(Galatians 6:10, KJV)

Affirmation: My cup is running over!

Scripture: *"Thou preparest a table before me in the presence of mine enemies: Thou anointest my head with oil; my cup runneth over."*

(Psalm 23:5, KJV)

Reflections

You can write your thoughts here.

_____

_____

_____

_____

_____

_____

_____

_____

_____

_____

_____

_____

_____

_____

_____

_____

_____

_____

_____

_____

_____

Our Children & Family
Meditate or Sing – Open the Eyes of My Heart
Open the Eyes of My Heart

Open the eyes of my heart, Lord
Open the eyes of my heart
I want to see You
I want to see You

To see You high and lifted up
Shinin' in the light of Your glory
Pour out Your power
As we sing holy, holy, holy

Open the eyes of my heart, Lord
Open the eyes of my heart
I want to see You
I want to see You

To see You high and lifted up
Shinin' in the light of Your glory
Pour out Your power and love
As we sing holy, holy, holy

To see You high and lifted up
Shinin' in the light of Your glory
Pour out Your power and love
As we sing holy, holy, holy

To see You high and lifted up
Shinin' in the light of Your glory
Pour out Your power and love
As we sing holy, holy, holy

Holy, holy, holy
We cry holy, holy, holy
You are holy, holy, holy
I want to see you

Paul Baloche/Michael W. Smith

Comfort

My mother, my mom, my mama, my hero, my protector, my guide, my Cleo

The worst and most painful loss I have experienced is when my mom had her sunset. She went into the hospital for what we thought would be a simple procedure. I traveled from Tallahassee back to my hometown of Hollywood, Florida, so that I could be there to help. She was talking one day and, in a coma, the next. What should have been a short period of recovery from a procedure turned into an extended stay in the hospital with months of rehabilitation.

Looking back, I realize that much time was spent away from my husband and children. While our mother was in the hospital, my brother Phil and I spent every day by her side. Eventually, she awakened and was transferred to rehab. We stayed there with her as well. Upon completion of her in-patient services, we finally brought her home.

I thought that my mother—my mom, my hero, my best friend, my listener, my supporter, my mama, whom my siblings and I lovingly called Cleo—was back. However, God had other plans. She left me to spend eternity with the Father. I truly miss her and the life she led, but I am thankful for her legacy. She is now God's heavenly angel but remains my enduring comfort.

Affirmations

Affirmation: All day and all night, angels watch over me and my family!

Scripture: *"Take heed that ye despise not one of these little ones; for I say unto you, That in heaven their angels do always behold the face of my Father which is in heaven."*

(Matthew 18:10, KJV)

Affirmation: My family trusts the Lord and leans not to their own understanding!

Scripture: *"Trust in the Lord with all thine heart, and lean not unto thine own understanding."*

(Proverbs 3:5, KJV)

Affirmation: My family is transformed because God has renewed their mind!

Scripture: *"And be not conformed to this world: but be ye transformed by the renewing of your mind, that ye may prove what is that good, and acceptable, and perfect, will of God."*

(Romans 12:2, KJV)

Affirmation: My family shows brotherly love!

Scripture: *"Be not forgetful to entertain strangers: for thereby some have entertained angels unawares."*

(Hebrews 13:2, KJV)

Affirmation: God keeps our family safe from all harm; his protection is always with us!

Scripture: *"He will not suffer thy foot to be moved: he that keepeth thee will not slumber."*

(Psalm 121:3, KJV)

Affirmation: Oh, come, now, Spirit Divine, and open my family's eyes so that they see you clearly and illuminate their understanding!

Scripture: *"To everything there is a season, and a time to every purpose under the heaven."*

(Ecclesiastes 3:1, KJV)

Quotes

"Truth is powerful, and it prevails." - *Sojourner Truth*

"It is easier to build strong children than to repair broken men." - *Frederick Douglas*

"Whatever we believe about ourselves, and our ability comes true for us." - *Susan L. Taylor, journalist*

"Character is power." - *Booker T. Washington*

Affirmations and Prayers

Affirmation: I teach and exemplify God's Word to my family!

Scripture: *"Teach me, O Lord, the way of thy statutes; and I shall keep it unto the end. Give me understanding, and I shall keep thy law; yea, I shall observe it with my whole heart."*

(Psalms119:33-34, KJV)

Affirmation: My children are an inheritance of the Lord!

Scripture: *"As arrows are in the hand of a mighty man so are children of the youth."*

(Psalms 127:3-4, KJV)

Affirmation: Lord, enable my family to establish a "Strong Hold" in you!

Scripture: *"The word is a lamp unto our feet, and a light unto our path."*

(Psalm 119:105, KJV)

Affirmation: My family has power, love and a sound mind!

Scripture: *"For God hath not given us the spirit of fear; but of power, and of love, and of a sound mind.*

(2 Timothy 1:7, KJV)

God Loaned My Children To Me

God loaned my children to me, and I declare and decree that no weapon formed against them shall prosper! I cancel every assignment of the enemy that seeks to destroy them. I plead the Blood of Jesus over them. They shall live and not die, and I declare the work of The Lord in the land of the living! They SHALL be successful, They SHALL prosper, They SHALL receive favor in abundance!

I expect and boldly declare it done in the Mighty Name of Jesus!

Amen.

Affirmation: My family and I submit to God; we are at peace as he does his amazing works!

Scripture: *"Submit to God and be at peace with him; in this way prosperity will come to you."*

(Job 22:21, KJV)

Affirmation: My family gives freely, for God loves a cheerful giver!

Scripture: *"Every man according as he purposeth in his heart, so let him give; not grudgingly, or of necessity: for God loveth a cheerful Giver."*

(2 Corinthians 9:7, KJV)

Affirmation: I decree and declare protection, prosperity & success for me and my family!

Scripture: *"Thou shalt also decree a thing, and it shall be established unto thee: and the light shall shine upon thy ways."*

(Job 22:28, KJV)

Affirmation: My children live prosperously because they obey and serve God!

Scripture: *"If they obey and serve him, they shall spend their days in prosperity, and their years in pleasures."*

(Job 36:11, KJV)

Affirmation: My family's world is blessed by God! Nothing Missing, Nothing Broken!

Scripture: *"The blessing of the Lord, it maketh rich, and he addeth no sorrow with it."*

(Proverbs 10:22, KJV)

Affirmation: My family and I are winners! We win!

Scripture: *"But thanks be to God, which giveth us the victory through our Lord Jesus Christ."*

(1 Corinthians 15:57, KJV)

Testimony

Everyone Leaves a Legacy

What legacy will you leave? Everyone leaves a legacy, intentionally or unintentionally. For me, leaving a legacy is teaching my children the Word of God by imparting healthy values, showing the importance of joyful giving, enabling them to respect themselves and others, and exemplifying how to honor and love the Lord with a whole heart. I am so blessed and privileged to have had the Bible as the principal guide for my family; thank you, God!

Many people will benefit from this legacy when we have a great vision and affirm Godly living for our children.

Affirmations and Prayers

Affirmation: Our family is redeemed from the enemy!

Scripture: *"Let the redeemed of the Lord say so, whom he hath redeemed from the hand of the enemy."*

(Psalm 107:2, KJV)

Affirmation: My children are taught Godly principles; they are living the Word of God!

Scripture*: "Train up a child in the way he should go, and when he is old, he will not depart from it."*

(Proverbs 22:6, KJV)

Affirmation: Lord, detox our minds so that our thoughts align with your Word!

Scripture: *"Let this mind be in you, which was also in Christ Jesus."*

(Philippians 2:5, KJV)

Affirmation: With love and kindness, I bring my family to the Lord!

Scripture: *"The Lord hath appeared of old unto me, saying, Yea, I have loved thee with an everlasting love: therefore with lovingkindness have I drawn thee."*

(Jeremiah 31:3, KJV)

Dear Lord,

I ask that you allow my family to wait for your assistance. Let them rely on You! Help them understand that you know them intimately and that you are completely capable of handling all problems, issues, and concerns. You are such a good and faithful God! I pray that they know this for themselves.

I love you, Lord! In Jesus' name,

Amen!

Affirmation: Praise God! My children walk in truth!

Scripture: *"I have no greater joy than to hear that my children walk in truth."*

(3 John 1:4, KJV)

Affirmation: My children's help comes from the Lord! They are amazing!

Scripture: *"But be not thou far from me, O Lord: O my strength, haste thee to help me."*

(Psalm 22:19, KJV)

Affirmation: Jesus saves my family from their sins!

Scripture: *"And she shall bring forth a son, and thou shalt call his name Jesus: for he shall save his people from their sins."*

(Matthew 1:21, KJV)

Affirmation: I pray continually for my family with patience and hope. I rejoice even when times are hard!

Scripture: *"Rejoicing in hope; patient in tribulation; continuing instant in prayer."*

(Romans 12:12, KJV)

Testimony

My Legacy Continues...

The Bible reminds me that material wealth can be just as important as intangible wealth. God's word shows me the importance of leaving goods, property, money, and riches to ensure my family's legacy. I affirm a financial legacy for my family in word and deed. Therefore, I leave my children and their children with financial wealth. I am putting together investments to ensure a financial legacy.

People will never forget what you did, how you loved, and how you cared. How you live from your sunrise to your sunset is your legacy.

Affirmation: Now is not the time to stop! As a family, we believe and remain steadfast!

Scripture: *"Therefore, my beloved brethren, be ye stedfast, unmoveable, always abounding in the work of the Lord, forasmuch as ye know that your labour is not in vain in the Lord."*

(1 Corinthians 15:58, KJV)

Affirmation: Oh Lord, teach my family your path for them!

Scripture: *"Shew me thy ways, O Lord; and teach me thy path."*

(Psalm 25:4, KJV)

Affirmation: My family is not lacking any good thing!

Scripture: *"The Lord is my shepherd; I shall not want."*

(Psalm 23:1, KJV)

Affirmation: My family is always thankful!

Scripture: *"In everything give thanks: for this is the will of God in Christ Jesus concerning you."*

(Thessalonians 5:18, KJV)

Affirmation: Lord, fill my family's cup with love; let it overflow!

Scripture: *"And thou shalt love the Lord thy God with all thy heart, and with all thy soul, and with all thy mind, and with all thy strength: this is the first commandment."*

(Mark 12:30, KJV)

Affirmation: My children live an unselfish life; they know that it is more blessed to give than to receive!

Scripture: *"I have shewed you all things, how that so labouring ye ought to support the weak, and to remember the words of the Lord Jesus, how he said, It is more blessed to give than to receive."*

(Acts 20:35, KJV)

Affirmation: My family serves the Lord with gladness!

Scripture: *"Serve the Lord with gladness."*

(Psalm 100:2, KJV)

Affirmation: My family has the favor of God!

Scripture: *"That in the ages to come he might shew the exceeding riches of his grace in his kindness toward us through Christ Jesus."*

(Ephesians 2:7, KJV)

Affirmation: My family has more than enough! El Shaddai is our provider; in him we trust!

Scripture: *"And God is able to make all grace abound toward you; that ye, always having all sufficiency in all things, may abound to every good work."*

(2 Corinthians 9:8, KJV)

Affirmation: My children live prosperously because they obey and serve God!

Scripture: *"If they obey and serve him, they shall spend their days in prosperity, and their years in pleasures."*

(Job 36:11, KJV)

Affirmation: I pray and affirm God's increase!

Scripture: *"The Lord shall increase you more and more, you and your children."*

(Psalm 115:14, KJV)

Affirmation: I and my family are free to live our dreams as God unfolds His plans for us!

Scripture: *"The steps of a good man are ordered by the Lord: and he delighteth in his way."*

(Psalm 37:23, KJV)

Affirmation: My family's world is blessed by God! Nothing Missing, Nothing Broken!

Scripture: *"The blessing of the Lord, it maketh rich, and he addeth no sorrow with it."*

(Proverbs 10:22, KJV)

Affirmation: The Lord's righteousness and benevolence have increased financial prosperity in my home!

Scripture: *"Wealth and riches shall be in his house: And his righteousness endureth forever."*

(Psalm 112:3, KJV)

Affirmation: We have the favor of God!

Scripture: *"That in the ages to come he might shew the exceeding riches of his grace in his kindness toward us through Christ Jesus."*

(Ephesians 2:7, KJV)

Affirmation: My family is happy, whole and complete!

Scripture: *"Beloved, I wish above all things that thou nayest prosper and be in health even as thy soul prospereth."*

(3 John 1:2, KJV)

Reflections

You can write your thoughts here.

_____

_____

_____

_____

_____

_____

_____

_____

_____

_____

_____

_____

_____

_____

_____

_____

_____

_____

_____

_____

_____

_____

_____

_____

_____

_____

_____

_____

_____

_____

_____

_____

_____

_____

_____

_____

_____

_____

_____

_____

_____

_____

_____

_____

Praise and Worship
Affirmations and Prayers

Affirmation: God loves me! This I know, for the Bible tells me so!

Scripture: *"The Lord taketh pleasure in me that fear him, and that hope in his mercy."*

(Psalm 147.11, KJV)

Affirmation: I praise God from whom all blessings flow!

Scripture: *"Let everything that hath breathe praise the Lord. Praise, ye the Lord."*

(Psalms 150:6, KJV)

Affirmation: Because of Christ, I am strong and can do all things!

Scripture: *"I can do all things through Christ which strengthens me."*

(Philippians 4:13, KJV)

Affirmation: Thank you, Lord, for your constant love, care, guidance and protection!

Scripture: *"The fear of man bringeth a snare: but whoso putteth his trust in the Lord shall be safe."*

(Proverbs 29:25, KJV)

Affirmation: Blessings and blessings and blessings; I am blessed! Thank you, Lord!

Scripture: *"O taste and see that the Lord is good: blessed is the man that trusteth in him."*

(Psalm 34:8, KJV)

Affirmation: My God, full of compassion, blesses and cares for me!

Scripture: *"May God be gracious to us and bless us and make his face to shine upon us, Selah."*

(Psalm 67:1, KJV)

Affirmation: *I woke up this morning an attractive, confident, respectful and loving queen. Every day my goal is to live in a way that is pleasing to God. I will rise and make my mark in this world by being courageous, amazing, and, most of all, Christ-like. I am determined to live fully and luminously. I pray that anytime anyone sees me, God is glorified!*

Monique Seymour- Payne

Affirmation: I live by faith!

Scripture: *"For therein is the righteousness of God revealed from faith to faith: as it is written, The just shall live by faith."*

(Romans 1:17, KJV)

Affirmation: The Lord is my shield and buckler; I am not afraid!

Scripture: *"He shall cover thee with his feathers, and under his wings shalt thou trust: his truth shall be thy shield and buckler. Thou shalt not be afraid for the terror by night; nor for the arrow that flieth by day."*

(Psalm 91:4-5, KJV)

Affirmation: I will humble myself, pray, seek God, and turn from my wicked ways; I will recover it all!

Scripture: *"If my people, which are called by my name, shall humble themselves, and pray, and seek my face, and turn from their wicked ways; then will I hear from heaven, and will forgive their sin, and will heal their land."*

(2 Chronicles 7:1, KJV)

Affirmation: My world is joy!

Scripture: *"His lord said unto him, Well done, thou good and faithful servant: thou hast been faithful over a few things, I will make thee ruler over many things: enter thou into the joy of thy lord."*

(Matthew 25:21, KJV)

Affirmation: Oh Lord, I praise You! I praise You with my whole heart!

Scripture: *"I will bless the Lord at all times; his praise shall continually be in my mouth."*

(Psalm 34:1, KJV)

Affirmation: Lord, open my eyes to see your wonders!

Scripture: *"These see the works of the Lord, and his wonders in the deep."*

(Psalm 107:24, KJV)

Meditate or Sing

"Here I Am to Worship"

My life is not my own

To you I belong

I give myself

I give myself to you

Here I am to worship

Here I am to bow down

Here I am to say that

You're my god

All together lovely

All together worthy

All together wonderful to me

- William McDowell

Testimony

God Is Real

Rather than taking an Uber®, I decided to call a family friend. He could use the money, and I needed to run an errand. When he arrived, he came in a pick-up truck instead of his car. I climbed into the truck and tried to close the door. The seatbelt was difficult to fasten, and the door wouldn't shut easily.

As we drove along a major four-lane road, the driver turned onto another four-lane road, and suddenly, I felt myself falling out of the truck. The fall seemed to happen in slow motion as if some unseen force was buffering me from hitting the pavement with full impact. In the midst of it, I thought to myself, This can't be happening, it feels too surreal.

It wasn't the kind of fall you would expect. I braced for the impact, but there was none. It felt like a dream, as though angels gently placed me on the ground. Then, I began to roll. I rolled so much that I found myself asking, Lord, will I ever stop rolling? But God had me—He was rolling me out of harm's way.

A woman driving behind us saw me fall from the truck. She turned her car around and reversed it in a way that shielded me from oncoming traffic. Then she got out and came over to check if I was okay.

At the hospital, every test came back negative. My husband called countless people, asking them to pray for me, convinced I must be hurt—but I wasn't. I felt fine. In fact, I showed no signs of having experienced any trauma.

That day, I knew without a doubt that God is real. What happened to me can only be explained as supernatural. No one can ever tell me otherwise—there is a God!

Affirmations

Affirmation: I sing praises to your name; Lord! Your name is great and greatly to be praised!

Scripture: *"Praise ye the Lord, for it is good to sing praises unto our God, for it is pleasant and praise is comely."*

(Psalm147:1, KJV)

Affirmation: Today, I let go and let God complete me!

Scripture: *"And see if there be any wicked way in me, and lead me in the way everlasting."*

(Psalm 139:24, KJV)

Affirmation: I am love, and I show love in all that I do!

Scripture: *"Thou shalt love the Lord thy God with all thy heart, and with all thy soul, and with all thy mind."*

(Matthew 22:37, KJV)

Affirmation: My world is peace; my world is joy; my world is blessed by, God!

Scripture: *"I trust in the Lord with all my heart and lean not unto my own understanding."*

(Proverbs 3:5, KJV)

Meditate or Sing

"Awesome"

My God is awesome, He can move mountains

Keep me in the valley, hide me from the rain

My God is awesome, heals me when I'm broken

Strength where I've been weakened, forever He will reign

My God is awesome, He can move mountains

Keep me in the valley, hide me from the rain

My God is awesome, Savior of the whole world

Giver of salvation, by His stripes I am healed

My God is awesome, today I am forgiven

His grace is why I'm living, praise His holy name

My God is awesome, awesome, awesome, awesome

He's Holy... Awesome...

He's Great... Awesome...

He's mighty... Awesome...

Deliverer... Awesome...

He's holy... Awesome...

Provider... Awesome..

- Charles Jenkins

Affirmations

Affirmation: God, let your anointing fall on me!

Scripture: *"I expect the Glory of God to be poured out on my life like the rain."*

(Zechariah 10:1, KJV)

Affirmation: There is wonder working power in the precious blood of the Lamb! God, has triumphed in my circumstance!

Scripture: *"And they overcame him by the blood of the Lamb, and by the word of their testimony; and they loved not their lives unto the death."*

(Revelation 12:11, KJV)

Affirmation: My faith is bigger than my fear!

Scripture: *"I sought the Lord, and he heard me, and delivered me from all my fears."*

(Psalm 34:4, KJV)

Affirmation: Lord, I bring every concern to you!

Scripture: *"Casting all your care upon him; for he careth for you."*

(1 Peter 5:7, KJV)

Quotes

"We have one life; it soon will be past; what we do for God is all that will last." - *Muhammad Ali*

"I am grateful to have been loved, and to be loved now and to be able to love. Because love liberates."

- Maya Angelou

"Darkness cannot drive out darkness; only light can do that. Hate cannot drive out hate; only love can do that."

Dr. Martin Luther King Jr

"The way to right wrongs is to turn the light of truth upon them."

- Ida B. Wells

Affirmations

Affirmation: I am redeemed from every work of the enemy!

Scripture: *"Let the redeemed of the Lord say so, whom he hath redeemed from the hand of the enemy."*

(Psalm 107:2, KJV)

Affirmation: Lord, manifest your power!

Scripture: *"And they overcame him by the blood of the Lamb, and by the word of their testimony; and they loved not their lives unto the death. Therefore rejoice, ye heavens, and ye that dwell in them. Woe to the inhibiters of the earth and of the sea! for the devil is come down unto you, having great wrath, because he knoweth that he hath but a short time."*

(Revelation 12:11-12, KJV)

Affirmation: I confess, believe, and receive by faith that all things are possible!

Scripture: *"For with the heart man believeth unto righteousness; and with the mouth confession is made unto salvation."*

(Romans 10:10, KJV)

Affirmation: God has worked it out for my good!

Scripture: *"And we know that all things work together for good to them that love God, to them who are the called according to his purpose."*

(Romans 8:28, KJV)

Affirmation: Joy to the world! The Lord is come.

Scripture: *"Every good gift and every perfect gift is from above, and cometh down from the Father of lights, with whom is no variableness, neither shadow of turning."*

(James 1:17, KJV)

Affirmation: I made it through - still standing! God has a plan for me!

Scripture: *"Being confident of this very thing, that he which hath begun a good work in you will perform it until the day of Jesus Christ."*

(Philippians 1:6, KJV)

Affirmation: Just when I thought I could take no more, God made away!

Scripture: *"There hath no temptation taken you but such as is common to man: but God is faithful, who will not suffer you to be tempted above that ye are able; but will with the temptation also make a way to escape, that ye may be able to bear it."*

(1 Corinthians 10:13, KJV)

Affirmation: I am praising, singing, and still asking why me, Lord? So much pain, but I have triumphed!

Scripture: *"But the fruit of the Spirit is love, joy, peace, longsuffering, gentleness, goodness, faith, Meekness, temperance: against such there is no law."*

(Galatians 5:22-23, KJV)

Meditate or Sing

"Praise Is What I Do"

Praise is what I do
When I want to be close to You,
I lift my hands in praise.
Praise is who I am,
I will praise Him while I can.
I'll bless Him at all times.

I vow to praise You
Through the good and the bad.
I'll praise You,
Whether happy or sad.
I'll praise You

In all that I go through,
(Somebody said why)
Because praise is what I do,
Cause I owe it all to You.

Praise is what I do,
Even when I am going through,
(See I've learned...)
I've learned to worship You.
(See I want to let the devil know tonight, even though...)
Though my circumstance doesn't even stand a chance,
My praise out weighs the bad.

And just go to praising him right now
Somebody lift your voice in this place
Lift up your voice in this place.

William Murphy Iii

Affirmations

Affirmation: God is so faithful; I will survive and thrive in 2025 and for years to come!

Scripture: *"But the Comforter, which is the Holy Ghost, whom the Father will send in my name, he shall teach you all things, and bring all things to your remembrance, whatsoever I have said unto you."*

(John 14:26, KJV)

Affirmation: Thank you, Lord, for wiping away my tears and giving me your peace!

Scripture: *"Hear my prayer, O Lord, and give ear to my cry; hold not your peace at my tears!"*

(Psalm 39:12, KJV)

Affirmation: The Lord made this day for me to rejoice and be happy!

Scripture: *"This is the day which the Lord hath made, I will rejoice and be glad in it."*

(Psalm 118.24, KJV)

Affirmation: Praise Him! Praise Him! God is great and greatly to be praise, You are worthy to be praised!

Scripture: *"Great is the Lord, and greatly to be praised; and his greatness is unsearchable.;*

(Psalms 145:3, KJV)

Reflections

You can write your thoughts here.

_____

_____

_____

_____

_____

_____

_____

_____

_____

_____

_____

_____

_____

_____

_____

_____

_____

_____

_____

_____

Prosperity

"Fill Me Up"

You provide the fire

I'll provide the sacrifice

You provide the spirit

And I will open up inside

You provide the fire

I'll provide the sacrifice

You provide the spirit

I will open up inside

Fill me up God

Fill me up God

Fill me up God

Fill me up

We need more of you, yeah

You provide the fire (come one, you say it, I'll provide the sacrifice)

I'll provide the sacrifice (you gotta tell him, say, "You provide the spirit")

You provide the spirit (I will, I will)

I will open up inside (you gotta tell him, "You provide the fire")

You provide the fire (I will be the sacrifice)

I'll provide the sacrifice (somebody tell him, "You provide the spirit"

- Tasha Cobbs Leonard

Individual Affirmations

Affirmation: My God meets all of my needs!

Scripture: *"And my God shall supply all your need according to His riches in glory by Christ Jesus."*

(Philippians 4:19, KJV)

Affirmation: Jehovah Jireh, I praise you! All of my finances are working together for my good!

Scripture: *"And we know that all things work together for good to them that love God, to them who are the called according to his purpose."*

(Romans 8:28, KJV)

Affirmation: I declare that money comes to me now! I cancel every debt and pay off every bill!

Scripture: *"For the love of money is the root of all evil: which while some coveted after, they have erred from the faith and pierced themselves through with many sorrows."*

(1 Timothy 6:10, KJV)

Affirmation: God, I pray that my eyes are opened to see your provision!

Scripture: *"The eyes of your understanding being enlightened; that ye may know what is the hope of his calling, and what the riches of the glory of his inheritance in the saints, And what is the exceeding greatness of his power to us-ward who believe, according to the working of his mighty power."*

(Ephesians 1:18-19, KJV)

Affirmation: God, make me a blessing!

Scripture: *"Give, and it shall be given unto you; good measure, pressed down, and shaken together, and running over, shall men give into your bosom. For with the same measure that ye mete withal it shall be measured to you again."*

(Luke 6:38, KJV)

Affirmation: I am strong and obedient; my riches are long-lasting!

Scripture: *"Riches and honour are with me; yea, durable riches and righteousness."*

(Proverbs 8:18, KJV)

Affirmation: My harvest has come!

Scripture: *"And let us not be weary in well doing for in due season we shall reap if we faint not."*

(Galatians 6:9, KJV)

Affirmation: Everything connected to me shall prosper!

Scripture: *"Sow your seed in the morning, and at evening let your hands not be idle, for you do not know which will succeed, whether this or that, or whether both will do equally well. In the morning sow thy seed, and in the evening withhold not thine hand: for thou knowest not whether shall prosper, either this or that, or whether they both shall be alike good."*

(Ecclesiastes 11:6, KJV)

Affirmation: This is my season of grace and favor to reap what I have sown!

Scripture: *"Every good gift and every perfect gift is from above, and cometh down from the Father of lights, with whom is no variableness, neither shadow of turning."*

(James 1:17, KJV)

Affirmation: Now, that I know him, I can show Him my seed in the ground; it's planted by living waters. I stress no more!

Scripture: *"And he shall be like a tree planted by the rivers of water, that bringeth forth his fruit in his season; his leaf also shall not wither; and whatsoever he doeth shall prosper."*

(Psalms 1:3, KJV)

Affirmation: I am rich, successful, healthy and happy!

Scripture: *"The blessing of the Lord, it maketh rich, and he addeth no sorrow with it."*

(Proverbs 10:22, KJV)

Affirmation: The Lord has made me the head, not the tail!

Affirmation: I am above, not beneath!

Scripture: *"And the Lord shall make thee the head, and not the tail; and thou shalt be above only, and thou shalt not be beneath; if that thou hearken unto the commandments of the Lord thy God, which I command thee this day, to observe and to do them"*

(Deuteronomy 28:13, KJV)

Affirmation: Lord, remember me!

Scripture: *"Remember me, O LORD, with the favour that thou bearest unto thy people: O visit me with thy salvation."*

(Psalm 106:4, KJV)

Affirmation: God's promise still stands, and I have an abundant life!

Scripture: *"I am come that they might have life, and that they might have it more abundantly."*

(John 10:10, KJV)

Affirmation: I decree and declare peace and prosperity!

Scripture: *"Thou shalt also decree a thing, and it shall be established unto thee: and the light shall shine upon thy ways."*

(Job 22:28, KJV)

Affirmation: I sow good seeds and reap good outcomes!

Scripture: *"I have a seed in the ground! Be not deceived; God is not mocked: for whatsoever a man soweth, that shall he also reap."*

(Galatians 6:7, KJV)

Affirmation: Today, I rejoice and receive! God has brought me into a wealthy place!

Scripture: *"Wealth and riches shall be in his house: and his righteousness endureth for ever."*

(Psalms 112:3, KJV)

Affirmation: I freely give and receive!

Scripture: *"Every man according as he purposeth in his heart, so let him give; not grudgingly, or of necessity: for God loveth a cheerful Giver."*

(2 Corinthians 9:7, KJV)

Affirmation: I am bearing fruit; my Lord is glorified!

Scripture: *"Herein is my Father glorified, that ye bear much fruit; so shall ye be my disciples."*

(John 15:8, KJV)

Affirmation: God's anointing is falling on me!

Scripture: *"I expect the Glory of God to be poured out on my life like the rain."*

(Zechariah 10:1, KJV)

Affirmation: I am fulfilling my purpose!

Scripture: *"I can do all things through Christ who strengthens me."*

(Philippians 4:13, KJV)

Affirmation: God, thank you for the great and mighty things I am receiving!

Scripture: *"Call unto me, and I will answer thee, and show thee great and mighty things, which thou knowest not."*

(Jeremiah 33:3, KJV)

Affirmation: My cup overflows with increased finances!

Scripture*:* *"Because thou sayest, I am rich, and increased with goods, and have need of nothing; and knowest not that thou art wretched, and miserable, and poor, and blind, and naked."*

(Revelation 3:17, KJV)

Affirmation: I praise God for all of His blessings!

Scripture: *"Blessed be the God and Father of our Lord Jesus Christ, who hath blessed us with all spiritual blessings in heavenly places in Christ."*

(Ephesians 1:3, KJV)

Affirmation: I rejoice, for the Lord has made me glad!

Scripture: *"Be glad in the Lord, and rejoice, ye righteous: and shout for joy, all ye that are upright in heart."*

(Psalm 32:11, KJV)

Affirmation: Thank you, Lord, for a new mindset in the handling of my finances!

Scripture: *"My God shall supply all my needs according to His riches in glory."*

(Philippians 4:19, KJV)

Affirmation: I fix my eyes on the right things!

Scripture: *"And I will give thee the treasures of darkness, and hidden riches of secret places, that thou mayest know that I, the LORD, which call thee by thy name, am the God of Israel."*

(Isaiah 45:3, KJV)

Reflections

You can write your thoughts here.

_____

_____

_____

_____

_____

_____

_____

_____

_____

_____

_____

_____

_____

_____

_____

_____

_____

_____

_____

_____

www.ingramcontent.com/pod-product-compliance
Lightning Source LLC
Chambersburg PA
CBHW060328130626
46553CB00003B/950